16322

£28

Signed
copy

RED KITE COUNTRY

RED KITE COUNTRY

A celebration of the wildlife and
landscape of Mid Wales

Photographic Images
by
Mike Read

Watercolours & Sketches
by
Colin Woolf

WILDeARTh
supporting
conservation

WILDeARTh is an imprint of
WILDGuides Ltd.

First published 2004 by **WILD**eARTh an imprint of **WILD**Guides Ltd.

WILDGuides Ltd.
Parr House
63 Hatch Lane
Old Basing
Hampshire
RG24 7EB
sales@wildguides.co.uk
Tel: +44 (0)1404 815383

www.wildguides.co.uk

ISBN 1-903657-09-1

Design by Colin Woolf Designs 01690 760308
Printed in England by **cip** Creative Ideas in Print Ltd., Stockport, Cheshire 0161 406 9300

WILDeARTh
supporting
conservation

RED KITE COUNTRY

CONTENTS

FOREWORD – by Iolo Williams

I was delighted to be asked to write the foreword for this book because it uses the unique talents of one of Britain's leading wildlife artists and one of our foremost wildlife photographers to convey the beauty of Mid Wales and the majestic Red Kite.

Central Wales has long been ignored by tourists and birdwatchers alike, the thousands flocking instead to the beaches of Anglesey or the mountains of Snowdonia to the north and Pembrokeshire or Gower Peninsula to the south. Wales' best kept secret is the so-called green void in between, a stunning mix of rolling hills, wooded valleys and spectacular wildlife. The heather-clad moors support breeding Hen Harriers and Black Grouse, the woods are alive with the calls of Pied Flycatchers and Redstarts, and birds which are reputed to be declining elsewhere in Britain, such as the Song Thrush and Bullfinch, are thriving.

Mid Wales is also the true home of the Red Kite, the most elegant of Britain's birds of prey. With its deeply forked tail, light head and rusty-brown wings, it is unmistakable, and while it was exterminated over a century ago from elsewhere in Britain, it survived here in the heartland of the Principality. Initially, a handful of pairs were confined to a few wooded valleys but gradually, thanks to the work of wardens, landowners and an army of volunteers, numbers have increased to almost 400 pairs today.

This bird is the British Red Kite, not the introduced foreigners which should be mentioned in the same birdwatching breath as Canada Geese and Ruddy Duck. The kite's success has lifted the hearts of a nation at a time when its coal mines, steelworks and national rugby team are but shadows of their former selves.

Colin Woolf and Mike Read have managed the unmanageable: to encapsulate on camera and on canvas the beauty and tranquillity of Mid Wales and its wildlife. With the publication of this book, Wales' best kept secret will no longer be the privilege of the few.

Iolo Williams

Wildlife Television Presenter

Newtown

INTRODUCTION – by Tony Cross,
Project Officer for the Welsh Kite Trust

For the greater part of the last century the magnificent Red Kite was synonymous with the rolling whale-backed hills of Mid Wales, having been eliminated from the rest of Britain by rampant persecution. The association was so strong that the area became known to many as 'Kite Country'. The story of the long battle to save the kite as a British breeding bird is as interesting for the clashes of personality as it is for the highs and lows of the birds themselves, and the lows don't get much lower. Successive 'Generals' in the battle were strong in their views of how things should be done and rivalry was commoner than the bird itself. In the very early days one or two of the so-called protectors even succumbed to the great rarity of kites' eggs themselves, unable to resist the temptation and perhaps feeling that it might be their last chance to secure a clutch of British kite eggs before the bird followed the Great Auk and Dodo into the history books.

Thankfully, the battle to save the kite is at last won, for now anyway. The kite has once again become a familiar everyday sight in many areas of Mid Wales rather than just an ephemeral glimpse. Feeding stations have turned kites into willing tourist spectacles, one of the few large and charismatic species, bird or mammal, that can be just about guaranteed to turn up and perform for the public, on time and to order. In this way the birds are finally repaying the protection and nurturing that the local inhabitants gave them. Feeding time is a spectacle that leaves few people cold, even those who have witnessed it many times before – up to 200 kites, with their five-foot wing-spans, swooping and clattering down to a meat strewn dinner table. Spectacular, marvellous, brilliant, awe-inspiring are amongst the superlatives that are repeated regularly in visitors' books. Kites are now adding substantially to the lure of Wales for many tourists and thereby contributing to local economies, helping to secure the future of some of the very people who have helped secure theirs.

The all-time low in the Red Kite population came in 1933 when just two nests could be located. This was after nearly 40 years of dedicated protection. It was not until the late 1980s that the kite population showed any great signs of a significant recovery. Prior to this the number of breeding pairs had crawled almost imperceptibly upwards from the stated 2 pairs in 1933 to just over 30 pairs in 1980.

During the 1980s, under the control of the 'Kite Committee' (foremost amongst its members being the 'the two Peters', Peter Davis and Peter Walters Davies), the conservation efforts to save the kite took on a new sense of urgency. Wardening schemes were organised, usually involving volunteer birdwatchers but also on occasions soldiers including Ghurkhas and the SAS on training exercises. Remote sensing equipment was tried – electronic eyes, pressure pads and surveillance cameras. At the same time scientific monitoring of nests by both the Nature Conservancy and the RSPB helped to explain why kites' nests were so unsuccessful. Armed with this new knowledge attempts were made to increase the population's overall productivity by 'manipulation'. Eggs were collected from nests deemed 'at risk', replaced with dummy eggs or Buzzard eggs, and hatched artificially. The resulting chicks were then fostered out at a later date to barren pairs and proven parents.

Add to this efforts to reduce persecution, through government anti-poisoning campaigns, and the benefits of artificial feeding, and the Welsh kite population was poised for a dramatic resurgence.

Concurrent with this, plans were being hatched, jointly by RSPB and JNCC (Joint Nature Conservation Committee), to re-establish the Red Kite as a breeding species in England and Scotland by transporting chicks from continental nests to release sites in both countries. These release schemes too have met with resounding success and enabled more and more people to experience the beauty of the Red Kite. However, for me, these successes are slightly tainted. In achieving that very success they have robbed the inhabitants of Mid Wales of the great pleasure of seeing their efforts through to the ultimate goal, natural re-colonisation from Wales. A Red Kite is a Red Kite when all is said and done, and we can only be pleased that the species is now faring so well, but it is very saddening when visitors to the area know little more about kites than that they were re-introduced into Southern England from Spain. We owe a debt of appreciation to the dedication of Peter Davis, Peter Walters Davies and the many other people in Mid Wales, both conservationists and landowners, who fought so hard to keep the kite in 'Kite Country' – the original 'Kite Country', that is!

Tony Cross, about to release a Red Kite back into the wild, after careful and dedicated rehabilitation.

The continuing fortunes of the Red Kite in Wales are monitored by the Welsh Kite Trust, a small registered charity formed specifically for this purpose in 1996.

ACKNOWLEDGMENTS

We are both indebted to so many people (and to the wildlife!) for allowing us the freedom to be able to produce this book. It would be difficult to mention everyone, but in particular we thank the many farmers and landowners for their permission to wander at will and of course the Powells at Gigrin Farm.

One person needs a special mention however: without the invaluable help and considerable assistance of Tony Cross, this book would not have been possible! We are both convinced that the resurgence of the Red Kite in Wales owes a lot to Tony's dedication, although he will protest otherwise! Proof of this is that contacting him proved very difficult most of the time, due to the fact that he spends so much of his time in the field.

We both would like to thank our respective wives for their support – additionally Jo for typing the text and for her proof-reading.

May 2004

OUR PURPOSE

For many people, the main purpose in visiting Mid Wales is to glimpse one of Britain's most beautiful raptors, the Red Kite. The sight of these elegant birds soaring over a wooded hillside is truly unforgettable, but, with our selection of images – evocative landscapes, fascinating detail and exciting wildlife – we hope to persuade you that there is even more to be discovered in this little-known area. There is a wealth of beauty to see and to be enjoyed in an atmosphere of utter tranquillity, and the Welsh people offer visitors a warm, friendly welcome.

Wildlife abounds in the area, and walking can be combined with birdwatching or looking for wild flowers. But sometimes it is worth pausing to look at the shapes and shadows of the scenery, or the details that are right there at your feet. Above all, whether you stroll along the banks of a rushing stream, stride it out over rolling hills or explore the beauty of the woodlands, quiet places are abundant here.

Much of what we have photographed and have seen has been on or very close to the road – demonstrating that you do not have to be a fit fell-runner to enjoy the countryside.

We hugely enjoyed creating the images (whether with the camera or on paper) – although the idea for the book actually came after the desire to take all the images!

Working alone, as artists and photographers often do, can lead to some highly creative images. Working together, however, enabled us to see each other's viewpoint and also find far more than double the images and beautiful things in this lovely countryside. We hope that you will get as much out of this book as we did out of exploring Mid Wales and putting the images together.

SHIMMERING SILVER WATERS

Rain falls frequently in the Cambrian Mountains and as the water collects in rivulets, streams and rivers, it begins a speedy, headlong dash towards the sea. The descent can be spectacular as the water navigates around boulders and rocks, through narrow gullies and over waterfalls. In good light, the water shimmers; it is fascinating just to sit and watch.

Full of oxygen, the water provides life for insects and their water-dwelling larvae that in turn become food for riverside birds like Grey Wagtails, Common Sandpipers and Dippers.

Within and beside the rivers, plants thrive and add to the glory of the place. Who can resist a prolonged pause by the rushing silver waters?

An adult Dipper feeds its babies almost exclusively on insect nymphs taken from the bottom of fast-moving streams.

Created in the early 20th Century,
the Elan Valley reservoirs are a haven
for wildlife as well as providing an
essential water supply.

From upland trickle to valley floor, the acidic waters look superb on a clear, sunny day. Even on dull days full of drizzle, it is worth taking a closer look at moisture-covered vegetation.

As the water makes its headlong dash towards the sea, it collects silt, grit and stones, eroding gullies through the rocks.

Whilst the sound of rushing water may drown out the song of Skylarks, its natural music can soothe our senses and create a mood of timeless peace.

A shaft of sunlight penetrates the clouds on a dull, rainy day, adding a sparkle to the Claerwen River and raising the human spirit. Rushing ever onwards, the fast-moving water smoothes the rough edges of mid-river boulders.

The meandering river and wandering road – both lead the eye through the upper Elan Valley towards a glorious sunset (opposite).

As river levels fall, plants are able
to flourish and this blooming Marsh
Marigold greets the warmer days
of spring. It is nothing short of
miraculous that this plant can survive
where rushing torrents scour the rocks
smooth!

Common Sandpipers return from their
African wintering grounds to establish
breeding territories along many of the
streams and rivers in Mid Wales.

An adult Common Sandpiper watches over its chick on a rocky shore. With so many natural hazards – rushing water, large rocks to clamber over or fall between and many avian predators – it is amazing that these youngsters survive at all. Their excellent camouflage does make them extremely hard to find and their parents are very protective.

On hearing its parent's alarm call, the instinct of a wader chick is to crouch down and stay perfectly still. This Common Sandpiper chick's superb camouflage is its best defence against predators. Have you taken a close enough look to see the chick below?

*An adult Common Sandpiper
bobs up and down patiently on
its watching place – making a
peaceful study for a reflective
painting.*

The River Wye, with its lush green banks, was photographed just a few weeks before the scene on the opposite page – striking evidence of how quickly water can disappear from the landscape, despite Mid Wales' high rainfall.

A Yellow Iris provides a splash of colour, its petals still fresh with the early morning dew.

The Elan and Claerwen Valley reservoirs supply water to the English Midlands. Following weeks of dry weather, water levels fall and mud begins to crack in the heat of the sun. At times like this, the lives of water birds become especially difficult.

Continually flicking its tail up and down, the Grey Wagtail lives up to its name as it daintily skips from rock to rock in search of food for its young.

A Pearl-bordered Fritillary enjoys the early morning sunshine. Once it is fully warmed up it will become much too active to allow the close approach necessary for a photograph.

The Silver Y (above) is a diurnal moth that is usually easy to approach and can be found resting on lichen-covered bark, where its cryptic camouflage blends extremely well. It is more usually seen feeding from nectar-rich flowers.

On the banks of the river, a moulted Mallard's feather still retains its natural waterproofing as droplets of rain stand proud of its surface. The stones, however, are coated in moisture, giving a lovely contrast of texture and detail.

Dippers have declined considerably in Britain in recent years but Mid Wales still holds a sizeable population. This decline is thought to be associated with changing water quality and a reduction in their food supply as a result.

Adult Dippers continue to care for their young for some time after they have fledged. Their method of feeding (walking and 'flying' underwater) takes a considerable time to learn. This youngster has a lot to learn and is still dependent on its parents for most of its food.

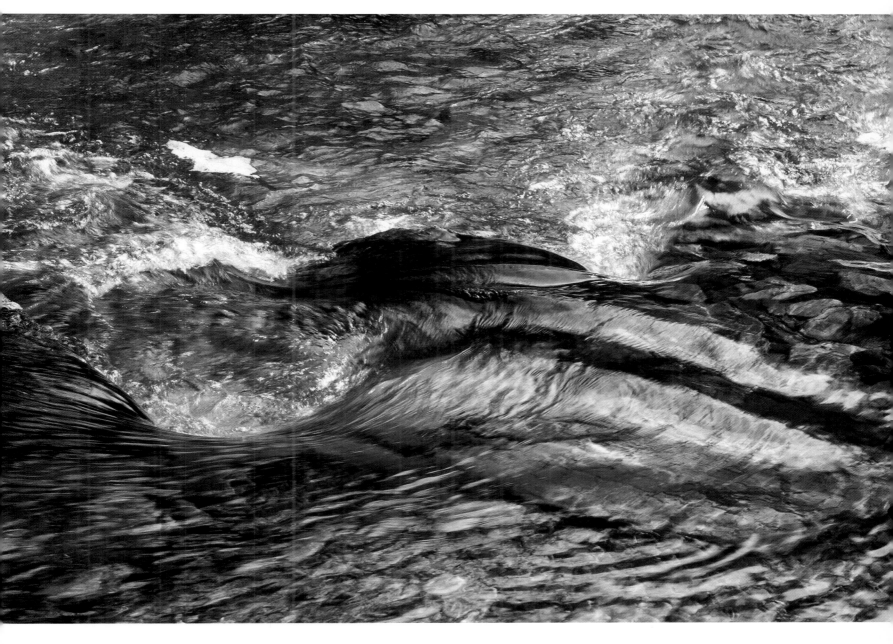

Some of the water shapes within a rushing river can make a picture in their own right.

As the morning mist rises from its surface, electricity-generating wind turbines are reflected in the River Wye.

The streams and rivers of Mid Wales hold populations of various dragonflies and damselflies including the Beautiful Demoiselle. This is a female; the male has bottle-green wings and body, all with a superb metallic sheen.

*Blooming Rhododendrons add a
beautiful splash of colour beside
Caban Coch reservoir.*

Darkening clouds over the Claerwen Reservoir suggest that the water level in the reservoir will soon be topped up. This female Teal rears her brood of ducklings in the quieter end of this expanse of water.

Pausing briefly before they fall, droplets glisten on a single grass stem. This is where rainwater begins its journey from hillside to sea or reservoir.

The petals of this Ragged Robin seem to droop under the weight of raindrops. Typically a plant of damper areas, this species has plenty of opportunity to grow in Mid Wales!

THE RED KITE'S REVIVAL

In the Middle Ages, Red Kites were a common sight over towns and cities throughout Britain but their fate was sealed by the passing of a series of Vermin Acts in the 17th Century, which wrongly considered them to be a threat to livestock and game. Many other birds with talons and hooked beaks were also persecuted, but the Red Kite was hunted to extinction in England and Scotland. They looked certain to suffer a similar demise in Wales, but somehow, in remote parts of the Cambrian Mountains, a handful of pairs survived.

Later, Red Kites were given a degree of protection, but egg-collecting still took its toll and severely hampered any possible recovery; unfortunately, this illegal activity continues to this day.

Genetic fingerprinting has shown that, until sometime in 1977, the Red Kites of Wales were all descended from one female blood-line, showing just how close these birds came to extinction. At that time, a German female joined the population, helping to increase the genetic diversity, and this, combined with increased breeding success in lowland areas, helped to achieve the milestone of 50 breeding pairs by the mid-1980s. Since then, Red Kites have gone from strength to strength: in 2003 there were close to 400 pairs in Wales.

This mother seems to be considering the fate of her chick; fortunately his/her chances of survival are much better than they used to be.

*A well-grown young kite awaits
the return of one of its parents
with its next meal.*

A pair of Red Kites keep watch over their nesting territory – a sight which, thankfully, is now becoming much more common. Even so, with a chick in their nest, they still need to remain vigilant for possible predation by Buzzards and Ravens.

With magnificent aerial agility, this beautifully-marked Red Kite easily avoids the aggression of a persistent Carrion Crow.

Very light plumage with grey streaks on the head and neck, and a pale yellow iris to the eye are distinguishing features of an adult Red Kite.

A moulted feather in late summer has its own intrinsic beauty.

It is in flight that the true majesty of the Red Kite is shown to the full. It is able to change altitude or direction with just a gentle flick of its wings or a twist of its tail.

A nesting kite's eye view of the interior of an ancient Sessile Oak woodland. This is the type of habitat which the Red Kites in Wales seem to prefer, although Silver Birch trees and Larches are also occasionally chosen for nest sites.

This alert juvenile (opposite) has yet to acquire the beautiful pale yellow iris and distinctive pale head of an adult bird. One day he may well be joining his parents in their supremely elegant flight – captured perfectly in this pencil sketch.

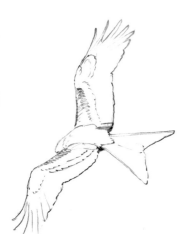

These lovely back-lit hills near Cwmystwyth have long been a good area for observing Red Kites. The late afternoon light picks out the few deciduous trees and makes the rolling hills, so typical of Red Kite country, stand out well against the background of conifer plantations.

It was near the Dinas RSPB reserve, Carmarthenshire, that one of the few remaining pairs of Red Kites bred a century ago. From here they have taken a long time to spread through the valleys because of their habit of returning to breed close to the place where they were reared as chicks.

'Watched from Above': in the depths of winter, two Red Kites search for a nesting territory while a Peregrine circles high overhead. This is Colin Woolf's tenth major work on the Red Kite, and aptly depicts the Cwmystwyth valley, where many visitors to Mid Wales knew that kites could often be seen – even when they remained absent from other parts of Wales.

SEASONS IN MID WALES

Whenever you visit the homeland of Red Kites, there is always something of interest to be found. Spring days can be quite balmy as leaf buds swell on the trees, ferns begin to unfurl and the first of the flowers burst into bloom. Soon the woodland canopy fills in and as summer reaches its full glory, less light reaches the woodland floor. It is now the turn of flowers in more open locations to bloom and set seed before the days begin to shorten and nights take on a chill that has been absent for some weeks. Morning mists cloak the hillsides as the golden glow of autumn begins, and much of nature shuts down or moves away. As rain, frost or snow becomes more frequent in the short days of winter, the Red Kites find feeding less easy. Kite feeding stations take on a much greater importance, especially for juvenile birds, as snow cloaks the higher land and the cycle of the seasons is complete.

For us humans, a wise attitude to the weather in the Cambrian Mountains is to 'beware' in all seasons: snow in the middle of May is not unheard of!

Two images of the same landscape, reflecting the sharp contrast of light and atmosphere brought about by the changing seasons.

Evening light accentuates the stunning autumn colours in the Claerwen Valley.

The Cambrian Mountains receive some of the highest rainfall in Britain, bringing life and beauty to Mid Wales.

By contrast, the water in the reservoirs can fall alarmingly low by late summer: compare the normal water level in the picture above with the level on the right.

Beauty abounds in Mid Wales and it is often difficult to decide which season offers the most attractive views.

*Ferns unfurl as spring brings
warmth to the ground.*

Heath Spotted-orchids (left) and Harebells (below) take turns to add splashes of colour to the green of the countryside.

Some of the hills in Mid Wales are cloaked in mixed woodland and scrub. With the arrival of spring, the willows are decked in catkins and the birch twigs show purple hues as their leaf buds begin to swell.

The blooming and greening of the trees herald the longer, warmer days of spring.

A narrow shaft of sunlight highlights the most gloriously-coloured piece of Bracken in the whole woodland.

On a fine autumn day (opposite), trees near the skyline cast shadows in the early morning mist.

Mist hangs over the calm waters of Craig Goch reservoir . . .

. . .take a closer look and the Raven mobbing a Heron becomes apparent.

A lichen-studded signpost encourages further exploration of this wonderful countryside.

Open, rough grassland like this provides ideal nesting habitat for many pairs of Meadow Pipits, which cunningly conceal their nests amongst the grassy tussocks.

*Clear skies, with the added benefit of no
'light pollution' from towns and cities, allow
the full glory of the rising moon to be seen as
it climbs above a typical summer skyline in
Mid Wales.*

The southern end of Tregaron Bog provides grazing for livestock and overwintering Wigeon (below) and Teal (opposite). Beyond, the slopes create good soaring conditions for Red Kites and Buzzards as westerly winds sweep in from the Irish Sea.

The wide expanses of Cors Carron (Tregaron Bog) provide ideal hunting grounds and roosting places for Hen Harriers in winter.

Careful searchers of the grassland areas in early summer may well come across this queen of orchids. It is the Greater Butterfly-orchid, now a rare sight – even in the unimproved grasslands of Mid Wales.

*During hard frosts, a coating of ice
forms on grasses in the splash zone
near some tumbling water.*

Sessile Oak and Silver Birch dominate this hillside near Rhandirmwyn. Although the photograph was taken in midwinter, the range of colours in this scene is surprising. In spring these wooded hillsides, where broad-leaved and coniferous trees give way to the moorland above, provide an ideal mix of habitats for many of our nesting birds.

Snow lies in hummocks over rocks in the Claerwen River (opposite) and covers the surrounding countryside in a magnificent winter blanket.

TAKE A CLOSER LOOK

So often on our visits to the countryside, we head out with a single, abiding purpose – be it walking, birdwatching, searching for wild flowers or a host of other individual things. However, in our enthusiasm, we often fail to recognise so many other elements in the natural world that surrounds us: things which we're unaware of, but which are constantly influencing our enjoyment. If we stand on the top of a hill and survey a magnificent view (easy to do in Mid Wales) our pleasure may be enhanced by a sweep of flowers in the foreground or the floating song of a Skylark overhead, even though we may not be fully aware of their presence. We may be unable to identify the flowers or the bird, but it is reassuring to know that they are there: our subconscious is lending a helping hand to enrich our experience.

Imagine, therefore, how much *more* enjoyment we would get from a walk or our birdwatching if we turned our attention to the things that we so often pass by.

In nature, we must remember that habitats and species are inextricably linked.

Make that link yourself by taking a closer look.

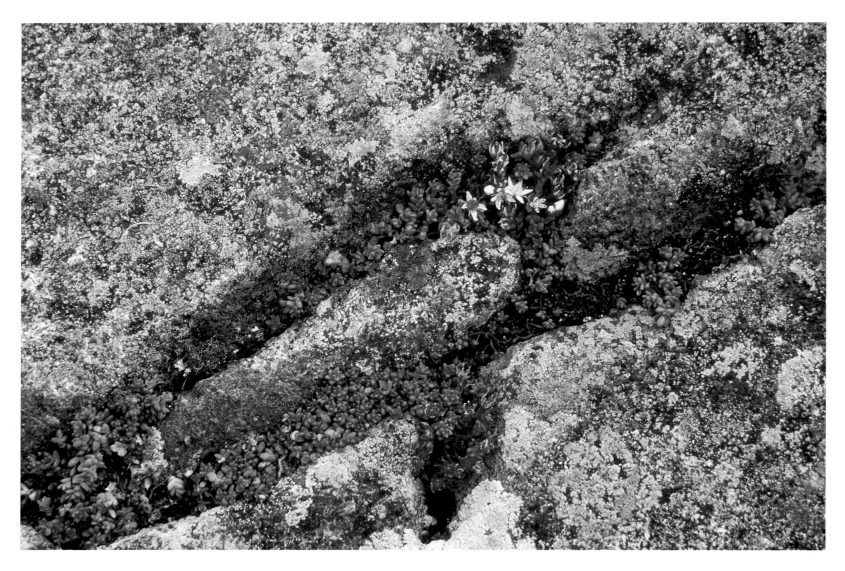

A small depression in the flat surface of a rock enables this English Stonecrop to grow in a place where many people stand to admire the view over a picturesque valley. But how many have admired the beauty of the plant and the lichens on the rock?

The constant trickle of life-giving water across a stream-side rock enables this Bog Asphodel to flourish in the most unlikely of places. Its normal home (as its name suggests), is amongst other bog-loving plants, rather than clinging to a rock.

A Golden-ringed Dragonfly hangs from vegetation in the early morning.   Being a cold-blooded creature, it needs to warm its body before it can hunt for its insect food or patrol and defend its territory against rivals.

The leaves of Navelwort, a fern
frond gently unfurling . . .

. . . and various mosses all deserve a closer look.

Although we may not like slugs in our gardens, they are a valuable food resource for Song Thrushes and Hedgehogs. But can they be described as attractive?

Whilst we can see the beauty of various lichens, mosses and other plants growing on rocks, how often do we pause and appreciate the colours and patterns of the rocks themselves?

A variety of mosses carpet the ground at our feet: a closer look reveals their beauty.

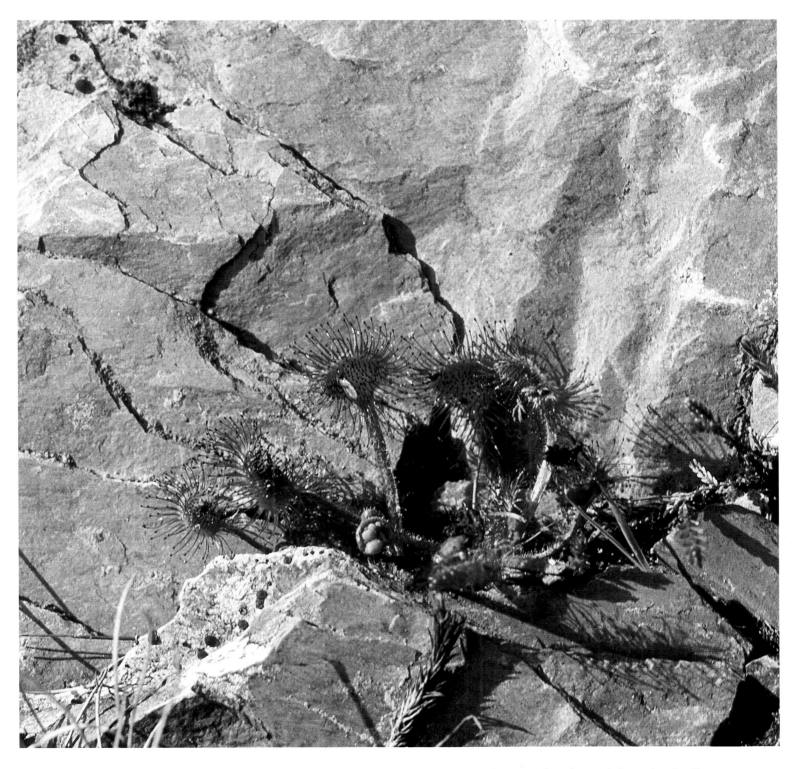

The Round-leaved Sundew traps insects with the sticky pads on its fronds, and then slowly digests them and extracts their nutrients. Typically a plant of boggy ground, it was surprising to see it flourishing here in a rock crevice.

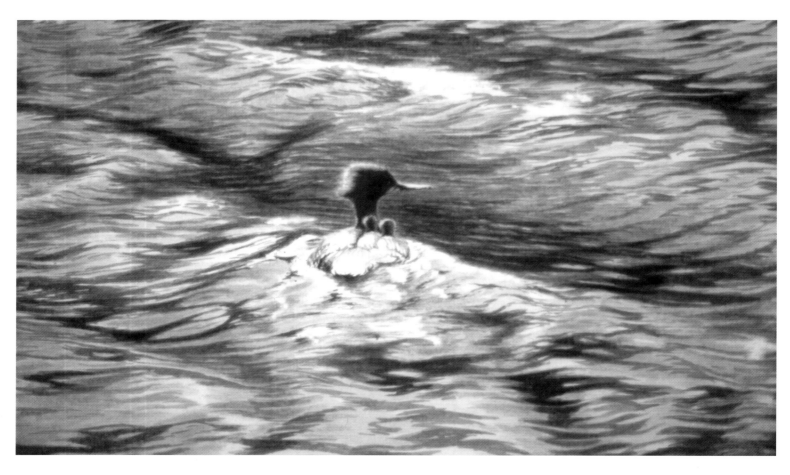

Goosanders are often glimpsed only briefly on the rivers, but the patient observer may be rewarded with better views. In this painting, a female Goosander ferries her remaining two chicks to safety on the River Wye, whilst the pencil sketch illustrates the striking plumage of the male bird.

A lone Common Butterwort clings precariously to a vertical slimy rockface. Like the sundew on page 73, this plant gains extra nutrients from insects that get trapped on its sticky leaves.

This Red Kite is itself taking a 'closer look' – in search of earthworms, insects and unsuspecting small mammals. Its incredible eyesight can detect the slightest movement, and its flexible wings and tail allow it to remain stationary in mid-air whilst it studies the ground beneath. This painting perfectly captures the elegance of the Red Kite in flight.

THE HANGING OAK WOODS

As the springtime buds begin to swell on the Sessile Oak trees, down in Africa many birds begin heading north to breed. When the leaves open and insect numbers increase, many species of migrant arrive to exploit this bounteous food supply. Guided by the sun, the stars and the Earth's magnetic field, three of these species – Pied Flycatchers, Redstarts and Wood Warblers – miraculously begin to appear and join the resident birds in filling the woods with song during this season of promise.

At this time, and on into summer, these woodlands are alive with birds, yet despite considerable research some intriguing questions remain unanswered. Once their single brood of young has fledged, Pied Flycatchers seem to just disappear. Weeks later, these birds (or are they birds from continental Europe?) turn up at coastal migration points, seemingly indicating a south-bound intent. Where they have been in the meantime no one knows.

As summer turns to autumn, many insects die with the onset of the first frosts and the birds which rely on them find it difficult to locate enough food. Many migrants now head south, while resident Nuthatches and woodpeckers change their diet and exploit the fruits and nuts produced by bushes and trees. Jays have developed a reputation as tree planters, collecting acorns and burying them a short distance from the woods. They cannot possibly re-locate them all, so their instincts help the continual spread of the forest.

Then we leave autumn behind and head to the cold, short days of winter when birds are busy finding food during the daylight hours. They have no time for song and only the briefest of contact calls are heard. Except for these calls and the sound of wind rushing through the branches and swirling the fallen leaves over rocky ground, the woods fall generally silent until another spring arrives.

Of the three British woodpeckers, the Great Spotted is the one found most frequently in the Mid Wales woodlands. Although capable of fending for itself to some degree, this juvenile (right), recognised by the all-red crown patch, will still be somewhat reliant upon its parents for food.

Dead and decaying timber provides a home for beetle grubs which munch their way beneath the surface. These are the staple diet of Great Spotted Woodpeckers, which use their stout beaks to chisel through the timber to reach them.

Spring is a wonderful time to visit these woodlands as the trees waken from their winter dormancy and become cloaked in fresh, bright green leaves. Birds, including recently arrived migrants, add to the atmosphere as they sing to declare their territories.

Before the leaf canopy closes and severely reduces the light reaching the woodland floor, Bluebells and other plants bloom.

A Bracken frond pushes its way up towards the light and, in a dark hollow close to the base of an oak tree, a Wood Anemone gleams in a shaft of sunlight reaching the woodland floor.

'A Welcome in the Hillside' – a female Red
Kite awaits the return of her mate with food
for their hungry youngsters.
This watercolour shows the ancient oak
woodlands which cloak the sides of the
valleys and provide ideal nesting habitat for
the Red Kite.

Whilst one kite heads out to find food, the other keeps watch over its nest. Many of the Red Kites in Mid Wales nest in the ancient Sessile Oak woods.

In summer, Pied Flycatchers breed in these lovely woodlands. Their natural nesting locations are holes in trees or in the ground, but an increasing number of nest boxes are put up for them each year, and these are readily used.

A male Redstart has a beakful of food for his young. This lovely summer visitor is fully at home in these oak woodlands, but tends to favour the forest edges where trees give way to scrub.

The myriad leaves provide a seemingly endless supply of food for insect larvae such as caterpillars. These, in turn, provide more food for the smaller woodland birds.

The entrance to this Redstart's nest
was much larger than normal,
making it more vulnerable to
predators.   Despite this, she laid a
surprisingly large clutch of eight eggs
and fledged at least six young.

Nuthatches are with us all year round and they make full use of the oak woods which cling to the hillsides of Mid Wales.

A young Nuthatch peers from its nest as it waits for its next meal; it will fledge within a day or two. Notice the typical way in which the entrance hole has been reduced by placing mud all around it. Nuthatches often take this precaution, thus preventing access by larger birds like Starlings.

The sun glints through the lower branches of
an oak tree on the Gwenffrwd RSPB reserve.

Earlier in the day a pair of Sparrowhawks,
those superbly agile hunters, were seen
performing their aerial courtship display over
this woodland.   After this, the male flew
off through the trees seeking prey.   Here he
pauses to look around and assess the best
direction for the next part of his foray.

As the evening sunshine illuminates the edge of a rock, it lends a golden glow to this autumnal scene and heralds the onset of frosty weather.

When it lands amongst light green foliage, the Green Hairstreak butterfly is superbly camouflaged and quite often goes unnoticed – but here it stands out well against the dark Holly leaves. It survives the harshness of the winter climate as a pupa, emerging with the warmer weather in April or May.

Now over a month old, this Red Kite
chick is well able to feed itself and
its parents visit the nest only briefly.
The full beauty of the kite's tail is
evident in this picture.

Every season in Mid Wales has its own dynamic appeal. In autumn, slanting rays of sunlight illuminate the burnished leaves of Sessile Oak trees, and the whole woodland appears to be on fire. Summer-visiting birds have already departed, and many mammals are preparing for hibernation. In a few weeks the branches will be stripped bare by the first winter gales – so take time to enjoy these glorious colours while you can.

ON HILL AND WILD CLIFF

Rugged cliffs etch their way into the rolling uplands which characterise the Mid Wales landscape.   Small ledges provide nest sites for birds like Peregrine, Buzzard and Raven. Nearby, among the Bracken and on open grassy slopes, Whinchats and Wheatears rear their young. Skylarks and Meadow Pipits make their home where the grass is thickest, but some still fall prey to Merlins and the rare Hen Harrier.

In some areas where sheep grazing has been less intense, heather moorland still exists. It is here that Ring Ouzels sing from cliff ledges (above and right) and a few pairs occasionally nest and raise their young. Red and Black Grouse also linger in places, although they can be amazingly difficult to see.

With such a variety of habitats, these hills and wild cliffs are alive with birdlife. But there is even more to be discovered: many plants and myriad insects can be found here too, all of which play an essential part in the intricate, natural ecology of the area.

If you are looking for a haven of peace and solitude, you will find it in these remote uplands. Take time to absorb the atmosphere, but also to watch and enjoy the wealth of wildlife all around you: it will enhance the magic of your experience, and you will become aware of the ever-present, natural vitality of this beautiful area.

As this fine male Ring Ouzel returns to feed its nestful of chicks, it pauses in a Mountain Ash tree. Despite the success of some pairs in rearing young, Ring Ouzel numbers in Britain's uplands have declined considerably in recent years.

Just above an autumnal woodland, a sweep of low cliffs, partly covered by heather, makes an ideal haunt for Merlins. Often mistaken for the larger Kestrel, they are our most diminutive bird of prey and occasionally reward the patient observer with a glimpse of their aerial prowess.

Close to their breeding cliffs, Ravens will often indulge in a fabulous display flight, each bird exactly copying the other's movements as they twist and turn, rise and fall – providing the inspiration for this painting.

Ravens generally prefer to nest on cliff ledges, but some choose to nest in trees. They are one of the earliest species to begin the breeding cycle.

As well as being superb fliers, Ravens have a wide repertoire of calls. In addition to their deep, familiar 'gronk-gronk' call, they can produce a range of notes including some which are fairly high-pitched.

Buzzards, like all birds of prey, frequently 'mantle' their recently-caught food to protect it from the eyes of other predators. Here the vegetation on the hillside is thick enough to conceal a dead rabbit.

Ravens are very intelligent but also cunning birds, and this one is trying to steal some of the Buzzard's hard-earned meal. The Buzzard is more than capable of defending its food, so the Raven's reactions have to be lightning fast.

When not out hunting, this male Peregrine would often rest on a cliff ledge near his nest. From here he could keep an eye open for danger, including the pair of Ravens nesting only about 50 metres away.

The female Peregrine leaves her small chicks only when her mate is nearby to guard them or when he brings in food. At this age, the chicks would be easy prey for a wide variety of predators or scavengers.

After a hearty meal, what more
natural thing to do than take
a nap, safe in the knowledge
that your parents are keeping a
watchful eye open for danger?

Later, the female's calls alerted one
of the chicks to another incoming
meal. The chicks on the previous
page are just 2–3 days old;   these
are approximately 3 weeks old.

As the Peregrine chicks approach fledging, they lose most of their down and exercise their wings more frequently.

Peregrines sometimes cache their left-over prey when food supplies are good. However, it is always in danger of being discovered by other birds, such as Red Kites, which are all too keen to plunder an easy source of food.

This sketch is based on observations of a Red Kite which stole the food cache of these Peregrines just below their cliff-top nest. As the kite made off with his loot, the Peregrines started calling in alarm and then mounted a concerted attack by riding the updraught of air and taking turns to 'bomb' the intruder. The attacks came every few seconds, and their assault lasted several minutes, but the kite remained airborne in the updraught and kept possession of the food, only turning its talons on the aggressors when contact appeared inevitable.

An increasing number of wind farms have been established in Mid Wales over recent years. Although they are a source of environmentally-clean electricity, they consume more energy and resources in their manufacture than they ever replenish with the energy they supply.

Their blades have been known to cause fatal injury to Red Kites, but more research is needed to determine whether or not they are a serious threat to migrating birds or seabirds that travel in flocks.

Whether we view them as an attraction or an eyesore, these turbines generate much controversy, especially when most visitors to Mid Wales come here for the views of unspoilt countryside.

A male Whinchat hunts from low perches to find food for his hungry young.

Evening light rakes across rolling hills where sheep graze. Red Kites and Buzzards patrol the slopes at this hour, in an effort to locate their final meal of the day. The morning and early afternoon are better times to catch a glimpse of a Peregrine out hunting its quarry.

Many bird species breed in the remote areas of Mid Wales. Some, like the elusive Snipe, spend all year here and yet often go unnoticed.

The Red Grouse was once a common breeding bird and a source of revenue for the area but now, like the Black Grouse, it is declining in numbers.

Wheatears nest in holes in the ground, including rabbit burrows, or under rocks. They are one of the first migrants to arrive in spring, with the earliest ones appearing on the hill by mid-March. Despite arriving so early, they rarely have more than one brood.

Young Wheatears often venture a short distance from the nest before they finally leave it altogether. This one is watching the slope where its parents are foraging for food. The first chick to beg is often the first to be fed.

These young rabbits by their burrow are fearful of danger. Their eyes are searching for the slightest movement and their ears are constantly listening for sounds that would betray an approaching predator. For some reason, they took no notice of the sound of the camera shutter.

Once a source of food for local people, about 50 years ago rabbits were wiped out from almost the whole of Wales by Myxomatosis. Now they are making a comeback, providing a welcome food supply for the rising Buzzard population and a not-so-welcome competitor for the already scarce grazing of farmers' sheep and other livestock.

Kites can often be seen hawking low over a hillside in search of insects or the occasional mole coming to the surface. They were once viewed by some farmers as a threat to new-born lambs, but a careful look at their feet will prove that they are too weak to fly off with large prey.

The small bird population – Meadow Pipits, Stonechat and Wheatear for example – are at much greater risk from the Hen Harrier (pencil sketch, left), whose low level, buoyant flight delights anyone lucky enough to catch a glimpse.

The peace and tranquillity of Mid Wales offers an escape, however brief, from today's increasingly hectic world.

FARMING THE CAMBRIAN UPLANDS

As winter gales sweep snow across the hilltops, the temperature plummets to well below freezing. The change in weather heralds problems for farmers whose flocks graze the Cambrian uplands. Now comes the mad dash to ensure that the animals remain safe and do not starve in these harsh conditions. Sheep are often moved closer to farms when bad weather is forecast, but in the rush some may be missed. Those that succumb to the severe weather will often be scavenged by Ravens, Buzzards and Red Kites.

Extreme conditions like this rarely last for long, and a rapid thaw usually follows. In these days of global warming, however, extremes of weather are becoming more frequent. After a fall of snow, the rush of melt water often floods low-lying grazing land, causing further problems for the farming community.

Financially, farming in this area has always been a struggle for survival. Recent changes in the subsidies system from payments 'per head' of livestock to payments 'per hectare' should reduce some of the pressure on farmers, encouraging them to diversify. This may work to the advantage of many upland birds, especially grouse, which have disappeared from many moorlands through over-grazing. If we revitalise the heather moors there will be tremendous benefits for wildlife, and the owners of sporting rights will welcome an increase in the numbers of game.

Visitors still come to Mid Wales to see the wildlife, and to escape into the peace of the countryside. This provides the inhabitants of Mid Wales with another opportunity for diversification: if we encourage more visitors to the area, the local economy will benefit.

It should be added that, to many birdwatchers, no matter how well the re-introduced Red Kite populations fare in England and Scotland, Mid Wales will always be true Red Kite Country.

A light covering of snow cloaks the higher ground around the upper Elan Valley and distant clouds threaten a further fall of snow.

There are few places like this left in Britain, but thankfully Mid Wales still has some large areas of wild, unspoilt upland which provide a living for farmers and also a habitat for many of our rarer birds.

Smoke rises from an isolated farmhouse on a still and frosty morning. Pickings for the sheep are meagre until the first growth of grass, which means that out here lambing sometimes comes as late as May. This typical upland farm has a shelter-belt of conifer trees to protect crops and the sheep at lambing time. During the main part of the year the sheep roam the vast area of upland.

Lower down the valleys, nearer the coast, natural habitats have long since gone; in the low-lying fields sheep thrive and some arable crops help to make farming more profitable.

Bluebells and other flowers can only flourish in areas where the sheep are excluded. Sheep graze much closer to the ground than cows, making it difficult for plants to flower; however, their root systems still survive and, if left ungrazed, the plants will flower again in time.

Centuries of farming have helped to shape the landscape of Mid Wales; with careful management, the beauty of the countryside need not be secondary to the profitable farming of the uplands.

In the grip of midwinter, a Red Kite watches a squabble between a Buzzard and a Crow over much-needed food. Snow can lie for many weeks on the upper slopes in cold winters and many birds struggle to survive.

The loss of the natural heather moorland,
which used to support large numbers
of Red Grouse and Black Grouse (right)
and other rare nesting birds like Golden
Plover (below), is a source of much debate.
The beautiful liquid, bubbling call of the
Curlew, once common, is now a rare sound
due to the draining of the marshy areas to
improve grazing.

Mist hangs in the valley below Glanllyn, near Rhayader.   The half-hidden lake and the ancient Sessile Oak forests that cloak the valley provide excellent habitats for birds. Very occasionally, Otters are seen here.

The soft evening light transforms an ordinary scene into something special, making the shadows seem like reflections in water.

The many old, abandoned cottages
scattered throughout Mid Wales
suggest a long-established decline in
the rural economy.

The increase in Red Kite numbers in Wales has undoubtedly been helped along by the establishment of numerous 'Red Kite feeding stations', like this one at Gigrin Farm, Rhayader.

The idea was conceived many years ago in Tregaron, and the number of feeding stations has now risen.

Without the odd sheep or lamb fatality to add carrion to their meagre diet, it is doubtful whether so many Buzzards and Red Kites would survive the harsh winters in Mid Wales.

The Irfon River rushes through the Abergwesyn Pass, a remote valley where farming is hard and the wildlife can live undisturbed for a large part of the year. It is not uncommon to see Red Kites and Hen Harriers hunting for food in this valley.

AUTHORS' REMARKS

At the New Forest Show several years ago, I met an artist who was using a Woodcock's pin feather . . . to paint a fine picture of a Woodcock!   We struck up a conversation, and from that day a firm friendship grew, and led to the production of this book – Red Kite Country.

During our time together in Mid Wales, I came to admire Colin's ability to see things that I did not. As a photographer, I concentrate on focus, exposure of film at the critical moment and the placement of the subject in the frame. Artists, and Colin in particular, see so much more detail as it actually happens.

This was especially brought home to me when we watched some Red Kite and Peregrine interactions.   Too far away to photograph, we stood and marvelled at the kite's ability to dodge and deter two Peregrines as they dived towards this territorial intruder. When the action subsided, we began discussing their behaviour but at the same time Colin began sketching what we had just witnessed. I was not only amazed at the accuracy of the moments his sketches captured but also the detail his 'seeing eyes' had committed to his almost photographic memory. See the sketches on page 103 if you don't believe me and then go on to marvel at the rest of Colin's sketches and paintings which more than adequately decorate these pages.

By the way, his artistic ability continues. It is Colin who has designed the book layout which I hope conveys to you the magic that we both see in Red Kite Country.

Mike Read

As a young birdwatcher I used to spend a lot of time trying to photograph birds, so I'm well aware of the patience and dedication required to achieve 'the shot'; but working with Mike has given me an insight which I wasn't prepared for – the amazing degree of personal discomfort which must often be suffered in the pursuit of a good photograph.

When we were in Mid Wales doing research for 'Red Kite Country', we wanted a shot of a Ring Ouzel singing from a high vantage point overlooking a valley.   We'd found an ideal site where the bird had been singing every evening. It was a scorching hot day in early summer, and after an arduous climb up the steep hillside with heavy camera gear, we arrived on the precarious ledge, with stunning views across the valley. Mike set up his camera, dismissing my suggestion of putting padding over the rocks that he had to lie on, and I carefully draped the camouflage over his prone form.

Arriving back at the bottom of the hill, I opted against waiting in the car after seeing the inside temperature was 45°C, and as the afternoon wore on I grew concerned for Mike's health as he lay motionless under cover in the scorching heat. At the agreed time I climbed back up;   it was nearly dark, and his camouflage was so good that at first I couldn't find him!   I removed the hide and he struggled to stand up; after so long in such an uncomfortable position, it took him at least 15 minutes and several bottles of cold water before he could safely climb down the hill. He'd had one foot hanging over the cliff ledge, but it was only then that he said he wasn't too keen on heights!

We didn't get the shot, despite further attempts; however, as I waited for Mike in the valley, I did get some close views of a Ring Ouzel, and these inspired the sketches which appear in this book.

In the many years I've known Mike I have realised that he has an amazing talent which many photographers strive for: the ability to see the hidden potential in his subject, and capture its natural beauty on film in a way that suggests a work of art.   'Red Kite Country' is a testament to Mike's extraordinary skill.

Colin Woolf

INFORMATION

Some useful sources:

Welsh Kite Trust: www.welshkitetrust.org
A charity dedicated to the monitoring and
protection of Red Kites in Wales.
Tony Cross (Project Officer), 'Samaria', Nantmel,
Llandrindod Wells, Powys LD1 6EN
Telephone: (01597) 825981

**Gigrin Farm Red Kite Centre and Feeding
Station**
www.gigrin.co.uk
Directions: On the A470, half a mile south of
Rhayader
Telephone: (01597) 810243
Kites are fed at 2 pm GMT (3 pm BST) every day of
the year. Also offering tourist accommodation.

RSPB Reserves: www.rspb.org.uk
Dinas & Gwenffrwd:
Directions: 10 miles north of Llandovery on minor
road to Llyn Brianne
Telephone: 029 2035 3000
Tourist info. (01550) 720693
Ynys-hir Reserve:
Directions: just off main road between
Aberystwyth and Machynlleth
Telephone: (01654) 781265
Tourist info. (01654) 702401
Carngafallt, Powys:
Directions: through Elan Village, 2.5 miles south-
west of Rhayader
Telephone: (01597) 811169
Tourist info. (01597) 810591

Tregaron Kite Centre and Museum
Dewi Road, Tregaron;   Kite feeding station at
Llanllwni, near Tregaron
Telephone: (01974) 298977 / 298415
Centre open Mon-Sat, Apr-Sept, 10 am – 5 pm;
weekends only Oct – end of March

Bwlch Nant yr Arian Forest Centre (Forest
Enterprise)   www.forestry.gov.uk
Telephone: (01970) 890694
Directions: East of Aberystwyth on the A44
near Llywernog. Open daily from Easter to end of
October 10 am to 5 pm (longer in summer).
Walks and picnic sites open all year

Elan Visitor Centre
www.elanvalley.org.uk
Directions: On B4518 3 miles west of Rhayader
Telephone: (01597) 810898
Open daily mid-March to end of October, 10 am
– 5.30 pm. Also offering tourist accommodation.

Gilfach Nature Reserve & Visitor Centre
(Radnorshire Wildlife Trust), St Harmon, Rhayader
www.westwales.co.uk/gilfach.htm
Off A470, 7 miles from Llangurig and 2 miles from
Rhayader.
Telephone: (01597) 870301

Tregaron Bog National Nature Reserve
 3 miles north of Tregaron on B4343.

Tourist Information Centres:
Llandrindod Wells: (01597) 822600
Builth Wells: (01982) 553307
Rhayader: (01597) 810591

Other useful websites:
www.wales-walking.co.uk
www.westwales.co.uk
www.e-britain.co.uk/tregaron
www.kitecountry.co.uk

Wind Farm Information
http://www.geocities.com/nigbarnes/#links
http://www.cato.org/pubs/pas/pa-280.html

INDEX to images in the book